Winter Mandalas
Color By Number
Anti Anxiety Coloring Book For Adults
– Seasonal Patterns For Relaxation

BLACK BACKGROUND

Copyright © 2021

All rights reserved. No part of this publication may be reproduced, distributed, or transmitted in any form or by any means, including photocopying, recording, or other electronic or mechanical methods, without the prior written permission of the publisher

Our Color Palette Tips

1. **Colors corresponding to each number are shown on the back cover of the book - NEW- There are only 25 colors total in this book, with one "Flesh Tone" color where you can choose any flesh tone!**

   Each number corresponds to a color shown on the back of the book. **There will sometimes be an asterisk (*) that corresponds to "Any Flesh Tone."**

   To the left of each image, there's a list of colors used within that particular image. Simply match the numbers on the images to the colors on the list. If you tear a page out of the book, you can simply use the color key on the back of the book to match your colors. If you don't have an exact color match, that's totally fine. Feel free to use a similar color or shade. Although this is a color by number book, it's completely okay to get creative and change up the colors listed. You can let your imagination run wild, and color the images with whichever colors you like and have. The numbers are here to be a guide and to allow you to color without having to focus your energy on choosing colors.

2. **If there are any spaces on an image without a number, you can go ahead and leave that space white (blank)**

   You can leave any space without a number white (blank), or you can fill that space in with any color you like. Another idea is to color that space in with a white color (for example, if you'd like to use a shiny white or a different shade of white on an image.)

3. **Bonus Images may have a slightly different color palette**

   Because the bonus images are from previous books with slightly different color palettes, they may include colors that aren't on the back of this book. Simply match them the best that you can, or choose completely different colors if you like. You are the artist and you are allowed to relax and enjoy!

Color By Number Tips

1. **Relax and have fun**

   Let your cares slip away as you color the images. Take your time. Coloring is a meditative activity and there's no wrong way to do it. Feel free to color as you listen to music, watch TV, lounge in bed- do whatever relaxes you most! You can also color while you're out and about- on the train or at a cafe- take the book with you anywhere you go. Coloring is therapeutic and is great for stress relief and relaxation!

2. **Choose your coloring tools**

   Everyone has their favorite coloring markers, crayons, pencils, pens- even paints! Feel free to color with any tool that you like! If you choose markers or paints, we recommend putting a blank sheet of paper or cardboard behind each image, so that your colors don't run onto the next image.

3. **Test out your colors**

   Feel free to test out your colors on our Color Test Sheets at the back, and use our Custom Color Chart to make the color choices your own!

   Relax and Enjoy!

5. Dark Brown

6. Tan

7. Peach

8. Red

9. Orange Red

10. Orange

11. Light Yellow

12. Yellow

13. Golden Yellow

14. Light Green

15. Green

16. Dark Green

19. Blue

20. Dark Blue

22. Violet

23. Pink

24. Vivid Pink

*. Any Flesh Tone

7. Peach

8. Red

10. Orange

12. Yellow

15. Green

17. Aqua Green

18. Light Blue

19. Blue

22. Violet

24. Vivid Pink

2. Gray

24. Vivid Pink

4. Brown

7. Peach

8. Red

9. Orange Red

10. Orange

11. Light Yellow

12. Yellow

14. Light Green

15. Green

16. Dark Green

18. Light Blue

19. Blue

20. Dark Blue

23. Pink

7. Peach

8. Red

12. Yellow

13. Golden Yellow

15. Green

17. Aqua Green

18. Light Blue

19. Blue

21. Lilac

22. Violet

23. Pink

8. Red

10. Orange

12. Yellow

14. Light Green

15. Green

17. Aqua Green

18. Light Blue

19. Blue

20. Dark Blue

21. Lilac

5. Dark Brown

7. Peach

8. Red

9. Orange Red

10. Orange

12. Yellow

15. Green

16. Dark Green

17. Aqua Green

18. Light Blue

19. Blue

21. Lilac

22. Violet

23. Pink

24. Vivid Pink

8. Red

10. Orange

12. Yellow

15. Green

17. Aqua Green

18. Light Blue

19. Blue

22. Violet

23. Pink

24. Vivid Pink

1. Black
2. Gray
4. Brown
5. Dark Brown
6. Tan
8. Red
10. Orange
12. Yellow
14. Light Green
15. Green
17. Aqua Green
18. Light Blue
20. Dark Blue

1. Black
5. Dark Brown
8. Red
10. Orange
11. Light Yellow
12. Yellow
13. Golden Yellow
15. Green
16. Dark Green
17. Aqua Green
18. Light Blue
19. Blue
21. Lilac
22. Violet
23. Pink
24. Vivid Pink

8. Red

10. Orange

11. Light Yellow

12. Yellow

14. Light Green

15. Green

17. Aqua Green

18. Light Blue

19. Blue

20. Dark Blue

23. Pink

24. Vivid Pink

1. Black

2. Gray

7. Peach

8. Red

10. Orange

12. Yellow

14. Light Green

15. Green

17. Aqua Green

18. Light Blue

19. Blue

22. Violet

23. Pink

24. Vivid Pink

7. Peach

8. Red

10. Orange

12. Yellow

15. Green

17. Aqua Green

18. Light Blue

19. Blue

21. Lilac

22. Violet

23. Pink

24. Vivid Pink

8. Red

10. Orange

11. Light Yellow

12. Yellow

13. Golden Yellow

14. Light Green

15. Green

19. Blue

20. Dark Blue

22. Violet

23. Pink

24. Vivid Pink

4. Brown
6. Tan
7. Peach
8. Red
9. Orange Red
10. Orange
11. Light Yellow
12. Yellow
13. Golden Yellow
14. Light Green
15. Green
16. Dark Green
18. Light Blue
22. Violet
23. Pink

24. Vivid Pink

1. Black
4. Brown
5. Dark Brown
7. Peach
8. Red
9. Orange Red
10. Orange
11. Light Yellow
12. Yellow
13. Golden Yellow
15. Green
18. Light Blue
19. Blue
20. Dark Blue
21. Lilac
23. Pink
24. Vivid Pink

7. Peach

8. Red

10. Orange

12. Yellow

15. Green

17. Aqua Green

18. Light Blue

19. Blue

21. Lilac

22. Violet

23. Pink

24. Vivid Pink

4. Brown

7. Peach

8. Red

10. Orange

11. Light Yellow

12. Yellow

17. Aqua Green

18. Light Blue

19. Blue

22. Violet

24. Vivid Pink

1. Black	17. Aqua Green
2. Gray	18. Light Blue
4. Brown	19. Blue
5. Dark Brown	20. Dark Blue
6. Tan	21. Lilac
7. Peach	23. Pink
8. Red	24. Vivid Pink
9. Orange Red	
10. Orange	
11. Light Yellow	
12. Yellow	
13. Golden Yellow	
14. Light Green	
15. Green	
16. Dark Green	

1. Black

10. Orange

11. Light Yellow

14. Light Green

15. Green

16. Dark Green

17. Aqua Green

18. Light Blue

19. Blue

20. Dark Blue

21. Lilac

22. Violet

23. Pink

24. Vivid Pink

2. Gray

5. Dark Brown

7. Peach

8. Red

9. Orange Red

10. Orange

11. Light Yellow

12. Yellow

18. Light Blue

20. Dark Blue

21. Lilac

23. Pink

4. Brown

6. Tan

7. Peach

8. Red

10. Orange

11. Light Yellow

12. Yellow

13. Golden Yellow

14. Light Green

15. Green

17. Aqua Green

18. Light Blue

20. Dark Blue

22. Violet

24. Vivid Pink

2. Gray

5. Dark Brown

8. Red

10. Orange

11. Light Yellow

14. Light Green

15. Green

16. Dark Green

18. Light Blue

20. Dark Blue

21. Lilac

22. Violet

23. Pink

24. Vivid Pink

*. Any Flesh Tone

4. Brown

6. Tan

7. Peach

8. Red

10. Orange

11. Light Yellow

12. Yellow

13. Golden Yellow

14. Light Green

15. Green

17. Aqua Green

18. Light Blue

19. Blue

20. Dark Blue

24. Vivid Pink

1. Black
4. Brown
5. Dark Brown
6. Tan
7. Peach
8. Red
9. Orange Red
10. Orange
11. Light Yellow
12. Yellow
13. Golden Yellow
14. Light Green
15. Green
17. Aqua Green
18. Light Blue

20. Dark Blue
24. Vivid Pink
*. Any Flesh Tone

6. Tan

7. Peach

8. Red

10. Orange

11. Light Yellow

12. Yellow

14. Light Green

15. Green

17. Aqua green

18. Light Blue

24. Vivid Pink

7. Peach

8. Red

9. Orange Red

11. Light Yellow

12. Yellow

13. Golden Yellow

14. Light Green

17. Aqua Green

18. Light Blue

19. Blue

22. Violet

23. Pink

24. Vivid Pink

8. Red

14. Light Green

15. Green

16. Dark Green

18. Light Blue

19. Blue

20. Dark Blue

21. Lilac

22. Violet

23. Pink

24. Vivid Pink

6. Tan

7. Peach

8. Red

11. Light Yellow

12. Yellow

13. Golden Yellow

14. Light Green

15. Green

17. Aqua Green

18. Light Blue

19. Blue

20. Dark Blue

23. Pink

24. Vivid Pink

1. Black

2. Gray

4. Brown

7. Peach

8. Red

11. Light Yellow

12. Yellow

17. Aqua Green

18. Light Blue

19. Blue

20. Dark Blue

23. Pink

24. Vivid Pink

8. Red

9. Orange Red

10. Orange

11. Light Yellow

12. Yellow

13. Golden Yellow

14. Light Green

15. Green

16. Dark Green

18. Light Blue

19. Blue

20. Dark Blue

22. Violet

ENJOY BONUS IMAGES FROM SOME OF OUR OTHER FUN COLOR BY NUMBER BOOKS!

FIND ALL OF OUR BOOKS ON AMAZON

Wonderful Winter
BLACK BACKGROUND
Color By Number Coloring Book For Adults

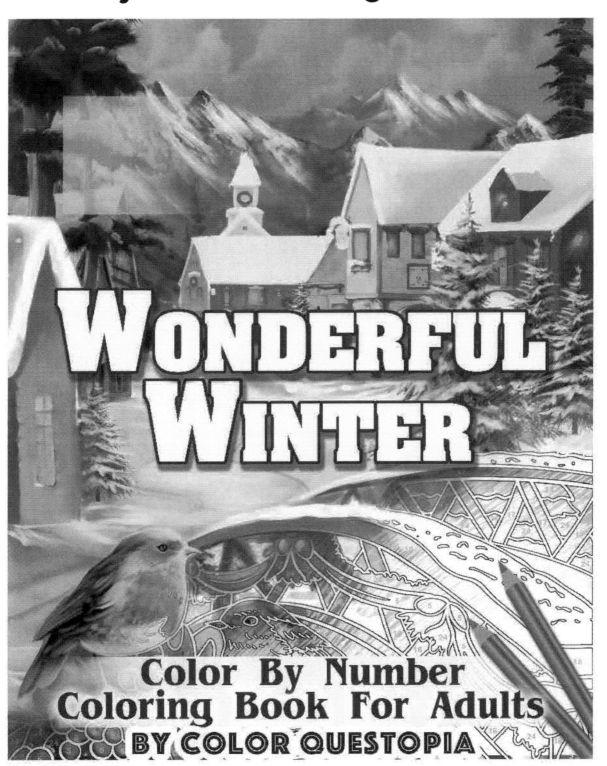

1. Black
2. Golden
3. Light Red
4. Medium Red
5. Red
6. Dark Red
7. Lemon Yellow
8. Light Yellow
9. Yellow
10. Dark Yellow
11. Bright Orange
12. Light Orange
13. Medium Orange
14. Orange
15. Dark Orange
16. Chocolate
17. Light Brown
18. Medium Brown
19. Brown
20. Dark Brown
21. Neon Green
22. Light Green
23. Medium Green
24. Green
25. Army Green
26. Dark Green
27. Peach
28. Light Pink
29. Medium Pink
30. Pink
31. Hot Pink
32. Dark Pink
33. Medium Purple
34. Purple
35. Light Violet
36. Soft Violet
37. Violet
38. Dark Violet
39. Baby Blue
40. Sky Blue
41. Light Blue
42. Medium Blue
43. Blue
44. Dark Blue
45. Navy Blue
46. Beige
47. Light Gray
48. Medium Gray
49. Gray
50. Dark Gray

MANDALA
BLACK BACKGROUND
Color By Number
Anti Anxiety Coloring Book
For Adult Relaxation

8. Red

9. Orange Red

10. Orange

12. Yellow

14. Light Green

15. Green

17. Aqua Green

18. Light Blue

19. Blue

20. Dark Blue

21. Lilac

23. Pink

24. Vivid Pink

1. Black
2. Gray
3. Dark Gray
4. Brown
5. Dark Brown
6. Tan
7. Peach
8. Red
9. Orange Red
12. Yellow
13. Golden Yellow
14. Light Green
15. Green
16. Dark Green
18. Light Blue

19. Blue
23. Pink

Angels
Color By Number For Adults
BLACK BACKGROUND

1. Black
2. Golden
3. Light Red
4. Medium Red
5. Red
6. Dark Red
7. Lemon Yellow
8. Light Yellow
9. Yellow
10. Dark Yellow
11. Bright Orange
12. Light Orange
13. Medium Orange
14. Orange
15. Dark Orange
16. Chocolate
17. Light Brown
18. Medium Brown
19. Brown
20. Dark Brown
21. Neon Green
22. Light Green
23. Medium Green
24. Green
25. Army Green
26. Dark Green
27. Peach
28. Light Pink
29. Medium Pink
30. Pink
31. Hot Pink
32. Dark Pink
33. Medium Purple
34. Purple
35. Light Violet
36. Soft Violet
37. Violet
38. Dark Violet
39. Baby Blue
40. Sky Blue
41. Light Blue
42. Medium Blue
43. Blue
44. Dark Blue
45. Navy Blue
46. Beige
47. Light Gray
48. Medium Gray
49. Gray
50. Dark Gray

Large Print Christmas
BLACK BACKGROUND
Color By Number Coloring Book

1. Black
2. Gray
4. Brown
5. Dark Brown
6. Tan
7. Peach
8. Red
9. Orange Red
10. Orange
11. Light Yellow
12. Yellow
13. Golden Yellow
14. Light Green
15. Green
17. Aqua Green
18. Light Blue
19. Blue
24. Vivid Pink

Custom Color Chart

Medium: _____   Brand: _____

1. Black
2. Gray
3. Dark Gray
4. Brown
5. Dark Brown
6. Tan
7. Peach
8. Red
9. Orange Red
10. Orange
11. Light Yellow
12. Yellow
13. Golden Yellow
14. Light Green
15. Green
16. Dark Green
17. Aqua Green
18. Light Blue
19. Blue
20. Dark Blue
21. Lilac
22. Violet
23. Pink
24. Vivid Pink

* Flesh Tone

Custom Color Chart

Medium: _ _ _ _ _ _ _ _ _   Brand: _ _ _ _ _ _ _ _ _

1. _____   2. _____   3. _____   4. _____

5. _____   6. _____   7. _____   8. _____

9. _____   10. _____   11. _____   *12. _____

13. _____   14. _____   15. _____   16. _____

17. _____   18. _____   19. _____   20. _____

21. _____   22. _____   23. _____   24. _____

* _____

Color Testing Sheet

Made in United States
Orlando, FL
29 November 2024

54651210R00054